# Practise

## Writing and Punctuation

### KS2 ENGLISH

# Age 9–11

## Brenda Stones

# Advice for parents

These days we are expected to be able to write fluently either by hand or on a keyboard, depending on the purpose of our writing. This book therefore gives lots of practice in writing activities, to help children think and plan, imagine and create through their writing. It can be daunting to start writing on a blank page, so these pages are devised to give your child the starting points and building blocks to get them writing. Extra paper should be available for longer writing tasks.

There is a whole range of writing forms represented in the book, from poems and playscripts, through fables and legends, to adverts and instructions. These are all forms of writing that children cover in Years 5–6 at primary school: the first half of the book being fictional forms, and the second half non-fictional.

Practising and checking punctuation is deliberately integrated within the writing tasks, rather than being taught separately, out of context.

- On the left-hand side of each double page is a model of a particular form of writing, to remind your child of the style, layout and punctuation of that form.
- On the right-hand side is space for your child to write their own piece in a similar style. But encourage your child to use their imagination and think of their own content, characters and contexts for writing. These are 'open-ended' tasks, so that each child can write to their own level of ability.
- Each unit ends with a further suggestion for writing that your child can do away from the book.
- The book ends with a quiz, to round up what your child has learnt.
- And finally we provide answers, to help either parents or children to check their work.

The most important thing is for your child to enjoy writing: it is a skill and a pleasure they will use throughout their lives!

First published 2007
exclusively for WHSmith by
Hodder Murray, a member of the Hodder Headline group
338 Euston Road
London
NW1 3BH

Impression number    10 9 8 7 6 5 4 3 2 1
Year                 2008  2007
Text and illustrations © Hodder Education 2007

A CIP record for this book is available from the British Library.

Cover illustration: Sally Newton Illustrations
Character illustrations: Beehive Illustration
All other illustrations: Simon Dennett at SD Illustration, Arthur Pickering and Kelly Gray
Typeset by Florence Production Ltd, Stoodleigh, Devon

ISBN – 13    978 0 340 94340 3

Printed and bound in Scotland

# Contents

# Welcome to Kids Club!

Hi, readers. My name's Charlie and I run Kids Club with my friend Abbie. Kids Club is an after-school club which is very similar to one somewhere near you.

We'd love you to come and join our club and see what we get up to!

I'm Abbie. Let's meet the kids who will work with you on the activities in this book.

My name's Jamelia. I look forward to Kids Club every day. The sports and games are my favourites, especially on Kids Camp in the school holidays.

Hi, I'm Megan. I've made friends with all the kids at Kids Club. I like the outings and trips we go on the best.

Hello, my name's Kim. Kids Club is a great place to chill out after school. My best friend is Alfie – he's a bit naughty but he means well!

I'm Amina. I like to do my homework at Kids Club. Charlie and Abbie are always very helpful. We're like one big happy family.

Greetings, readers, my name's Alfie! Everybody knows me here. Come and join our club; we'll have a wicked time together!

Now you've met us all, tell us something about yourself.
All the kids filled in a '**Personal Profile**' when they joined. Here's one for you to complete.

## Personal Profile

INSERT PHOTO OF YOURSELF HERE

Name: ______________________________

Age: ____

School: ____________________________

Home town: ___________________________

Best friend: ___________________

My favourite:

- Book __________________
- Film __________________
- Food __________________
- Sport __________________

My hero is ________________ because ________________

______________________________________________________

When I grow up I want to be a _________________________

If I ruled the world the first thing I would do is _____________

______________________________________________________

If I could be any celebrity for a day I would be _____________

______________________________________________________

# 1: Write a poem

Do you know what a **limerick** is? It's usually a funny poem, which follows the pattern of lines and rhymes of the examples below.

One poet who wrote a lot of limericks was Edward Lear. His first book of 'nonsense verse' came out in 1846. Here are two of his limericks.

There was an old person of Dean,
Who dined on one pea and one bean;
    For he said, "More than that
    Would make me too fat,"
That cautious old person of Dean.

There was an old person in grey,
Whose feelings were tinged with dismay;
    She purchased two parrots,
    And fed them with carrots,
Which pleased that old person in grey.

## Get ready

1. How many lines do limericks have? _____

2. How many syllables do they have in each line? _____

3. Which lines rhyme? _____

4. In which lines are phrases repeated? _____

## Let's practise

Now you try writing a limerick.

You could make it start:
'There was a young girl/boy . . .'

Make sure you follow the lines and
the rhyme patterns opposite.

_____

_____

_____

_____

_____

## Have a go

Search for limericks on the Internet.
Which are the funniest you find?
Do they all follow the same pattern?

# 2: Write a playscript

Do you ever spend time listening to what people really say in conversation?

To write a scene for a play, you need to separate what people say (the **speech**) from what they do (the **stage directions**).

Read this example, looking at what's in the speech, and what's in the stage directions or actions.

---

[*The family are seated round the table.* AUNT FORD *is serving roast lamb to her nephews.*]
AUNT FORD: Sam, would you like some roast lamb, with potatoes and caper sauce?
SAM: Yes please, Aunt.
[AUNT FORD *gives him a good portion, and he wolfs it down.*]

AUNT FORD: Would you like some more, Sam?
SAM: Yes, please. I'd like a huge helping, a monster helping, a ginormous helping, please!
MUM: Careful, Sam!
[SAM *finishes this portion as well.*]

AUNT FORD: Sam, could you eat another helping?
MUM: Sam, you know that enough is as good as a feast.
SAM: No, I think that *too much* is the only thing that's as good as a feast!
[SAM *starts to eat, but begins to look a bit ill as he keeps eating . . .*]

---

## Get ready

**1** How are the stage directions written? _____

**2** What tense are they written in? _____

**3** How are the characters' names written? _____

**4** Are there any speech marks in playscripts? _____

**5** What makes the plot move forward, the speech or the stage directions? _____

## Let's practise

Write a part of a playscript.

You could start by listening to what people say on the bus, or in a TV drama or soap.

Then decide what goes in the speech, and what goes in the stage directions.

_____

_____

_____

_____

_____

_____

_____

## Have a go

Try recording a bit of conversation at home, and then write it down.
Lay it out as in the example opposite.

# 3: Punctuate speech

There are other ways we could write the speeches from the playscript in Unit 2.

If we turned them into **direct speech** in a story, they'd read like this:

"Sam, would you like some roast lamb, with potatoes and caper sauce?" asked Aunt Ford.

"Yes please, Aunt," he replied.

She served him a good portion, and he wolfed it down.

She then asked, "Would you like some more, Sam?"

"Yes, please," he said. "I'd like a huge helping, a monster helping, a ginormous helping, please!"

Mum began to get anxious: "Careful, Sam!"

But Sam finished that portion as well.

When Aunt Ford asked, "Sam, could you eat another helping?" Mum got really anxious.

"Sam, you know that enough is as good as a feast."

But Sam's answer was, "No, I think that *too much* is the only thing that's as good as a feast!"

## Get ready

**1** What punctuation has been added? _____

**2** Does the punctuation at the end of each speech go inside or outside the speech marks? _____

**3** When do you start a new line? _____

**4** What different verbs are used instead of 'said'? _____

**Let's practise**

Another way of writing speech is **reported speech**. This means that you relate what was said, but not in speech marks.

Look at the example below, where I have started to write out the dialogue opposite in reported speech. Continue writing the rest of the passage in the same way. You will need to use a separate piece of paper to complete the passage.

Aunt Ford asked Sam whether he'd like some roast lamb, with potatoes and caper sauce.

He said eagerly that he would . . . _____

_____

_____

_____

_____

_____

_____

**Have a go**

Write a whole conversation in three forms: as a playscript, as direct speech and as reported speech. Which version works best, do you feel? Why?

# 4: Plan and write a story

Have you used this 'Y plan' before, for planning a story?

It helps you think through the characters and the setting, before you get on to the beginning, middle and ending of the plot.

| Characters | Setting |
|---|---|
| The merchant and his wife | Holland, a few centuries ago, when people grew prize tulip bulbs |

**Beginning**
The merchant develops a prize-winning bulb.

**Middle**
The merchant's wife goes out to the kitchen to prepare dinner.

**Ending**
What does the merchant discover?

## Get ready

**1** What do you predict might happen from this plan?

_____

**2** In particular, what might happen when the merchant's wife goes to prepare dinner? _____

 **Let's practise**

Write out your own version of the story in Megan's plan.

Give your story at least three paragraphs, one each for the beginning, the middle and the ending. Start here with a paragraph or two as an introduction, to describe the setting and the characters. You may need to continue on a separate piece of paper.

 **Have a go**

Research more about this period in Holland, when tulip bulbs were so valuable. See if you can find the names of some famous Dutch artists of the time.

Here's our version of the whole story, from the plan in Unit 4.

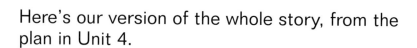

There was once a merchant and his wife, who lived in Holland many centuries ago. This was the time when tulip bulbs were terribly valuable, because everyone wanted to see different kinds of tulips: plain colours, patterned colours, stripes and fluted petals. The best tulips used to raise thousands of gilders!

This merchant was especially good at growing tulips. He was breeding the bulbs, and developing the best colour combinations in the whole of Holland. He kept them in the dark under the stairs, but occasionally brought them out when he was ready to put them in for prizes. And this was what he did one winter's evening, when he was getting ready for the biggest awards of the year.

That evening the merchant's wife was in a hurry to prepare dinner, as she was going out to lace-making classes as soon as she'd done the washing up. So she didn't even bother to light the lamp in the kitchen, but just chopped up all the ingredients for a stew and put it on to simmer.

Just imagine what the merchant felt when he went into the kitchen after his wife had gone out, and searched for the prize bulb he'd put out ready. Just imagine his language when he found the onion peelings in the bin. No, they weren't onion peelings, it was the skin of his prize tulip bulb, skulking at the bottom of the bin with all the leftovers from dinner . . .

## Get ready

**1** Is this what you expected from the plan?

_____

**2** How does it compare with your version of the story?

_____

**3** Which bits are better or worse than yours?

_____

##  Let's practise

Let's imagine a more cheerful ending to the story. Let's imagine that something different happened when the merchant's wife went out to the kitchen.

Write an **alternative** ending to the story, one that leaves the merchant able to enter his prize bulb for the Top Tulip Awards.

_____

_____

_____

_____

_____

_____

_____

##  Have a go

Think of a traditional story that has a sad ending, like the Pied Piper of Hamelin. Rewrite the story with a happy ending. Which version works better? Why?

# 6: Write a fable

Do you know what a **fable** is? It's a story with a moral at the end, which means it has a message about what you should do in life.

Fables are usually written about animals, to make the message simple. Here's an example:

There was once a lioness and her cubs. The first cub was boisterous, and often fell into streams and ditches. The second cub was always careful and obedient, and rather boring. The third cub was so shy that he never let go of his mother's tail.

One day they went off hunting in the bush, hoping to catch a small deer.

"There's one," said the lioness. "See if you can catch it!"

The first cub gave a great whoop and leaped so high that he fell into the river, and frightened the small deer away.

The third cub started wailing, and hid behind a large cactus.

The second cub waited patiently and then tracked down the deer so that they could all eat supper.

**Moral**: Look before you leap. (But life would be boring if we were all the same!)

## Get ready

**1**  How does the first sentence suggest that this is not a factual account?

_____

**2**  Why are there three cubs?

_____

**3**  Who is the only character to use direct speech?

_____

**4**  Which phrases give humour to the story?

_____

**5**  What other wording could you use for the moral of the fable?

_____

## Let's practise

Now you write a fable, using animals as the characters.

You'll probably need to think up your moral first, so you can write your story round it.

_____

_____

_____

_____

_____

_____

_____

**Moral**: _____

## Have a go

Find some fables written by Aesop, who was an ancient Greek, or by La Fontaine, who was a French writer. Then write a modern version of one of them, using people rather than animals.

# 7: Rewrite a legend

Can you define what a **legend** is? It's a story handed down from the past, which may not be true in its details, but has important truths to tell us.

Read this brief version of the legend of Sir Gawain and the Green Knight.

One Christmas, King Arthur and his knights of the Round Table were sitting round a feast in Camelot. Suddenly, in rode a green knight on a green horse, and challenged King Arthur's men to test their bravery and their honour. The youngest knight was Sir Gawain, and he rose to accept the challenge. The green knight told Gawain to chop off his head, but to return in a year to have the same done to him. Gawain did the deed, to prove his bravery, and the green knight rode off with his head tucked underneath his arm.

A year later, Gawain rode off to find the green knight and keep his promise. He found a magical castle in a wood, and was invited to stay the night. Three times the lady of the castle visited Gawain to tempt him, but three times he kept his honour. In the end he accepted her green belt, to keep him safe.

Gawain then rode on and found the green knight, who three times raised his sword to chop off Gawain's head. But he spared Gawain, in recognition of the three times that Gawain had resisted his wife. The green knight let him keep the green belt, in memory of the trial of his chivalry, and Gawain returned to Arthur, to narrate his adventure.

## Get ready

**1** Do you think King Arthur and Sir Gawain really existed?

_____

**2** Do you think that the green knight really existed?

_____

**3** Which qualities of knightly behaviour was the green knight testing?

_____

**4** Why was Gawain spared three times?

_____

## Let's practise

Try rewriting this legend as a modern story. You should keep the elements of being tested for bravery, and keeping your honour. But make the setting and the characters modern. You will need to continue on a separate piece of paper.

_____

_____

_____

_____

_____

_____

_____

## Have a go

Find more legends about King Arthur and his knights of the Round Table.

Find more versions of the Sir Gawain story, for instance in the long poem by Tennyson.

Research the history of Camelot on the Internet.

Shakespeare's plays are really difficult to read, aren't they? Luckily, however, there are lots of retellings of the plays that make the stories easier to understand.

Here's just a bit from *Romeo and Juliet*, which we've managed to explain in modern English.

| | |
|---|---|
| **Juliet** | |
| How camest thou hither, tell me, and wherefore? | How did you get here? |
| The orchard walls are high and hard to climb, | The orchard walls are high and hard to climb, |
| And the place death, considering who thou art, | And dangerous, considering who you are, |
| If any of my kinsmen find thee here. | If any of my family find you here. |
| | |
| **Romeo** | |
| With love's light wings did I o'erperch these walls; | Love helped me climb the walls; |
| For stony limits cannot hold love out, | These stones can't keep love out, |
| And what love can do, that dares love attempt: | Love will dare to do anything, |
| Therefore thy kinsmen are no stop to me. | So your family are not about to stop me. |

## Get ready

1  Which version was easier to understand?

_____

2  Which version had more poetic langage?

_____

3  Does it help to read the Shakespeare version aloud?

_____

## Let's practise

The following speech is from the same play. Try to explain in modern English what the Nurse is saying.

| Nurse | |
| --- | --- |
| Now afore God, I am so vexed that every part about me quivers. Scurvy knave! Pray you, sir, a word. And as I told you, my young lady bid me enquire you out. What she bid me say I will keep to myself: but first let me tell ye, if ye should lead her in a fool's paradise, as they say, it were a very gross kind of behaviour, as they say: for the gentlewoman is young; and therefore, if you should deal double with her, truly it were an ill thing to be offered to any gentlewoman, and very weak dealing. | _____ |

## Have a go

Find some retellings of Shakespeare's plays; there are some great versions in cartoon strips! Try comparing them with the original text, so that you can work out what the original words mean.

# 9: Compare a book and a film

Have any of your favourite books been made into films? Which version did you prefer? Why?

Here's a chart to help you work out what you prefer about each version. We've filled in this one for *Jane Eyre*.

| Prefer about the book | Dislike in the film |
|---|---|
| Jane is short and plain | Jane is too tall and too pretty |
| Rochester is a brooding character | Rochester is too good-looking |
| **Dislike about the book** | **Prefer in the film** |
| Long to read | Shorter in film |
| | Film settings in Derbyshire |
| | Dramatic contrasts of light and shade |

## Get ready

1 Do you create pictures of the characters in your head, when you read?

2 Does the setting of a film help you imagine the landscape?

3 Do you notice the music they use for film scores?

### Let's practise

Compare the film version with a book that you've read, for example a Harry Potter book or *Lord of the Rings*, or a Roald Dahl story. Use the same chart to help you.

| Prefer about the book | Dislike in the film |
|---|---|
| | |
| Dislike about the book | Prefer in the film |
| | |

### Have a go

Find a review of a film of a book, where you know both versions. Do you agree with the review, or do you have a different opinion?

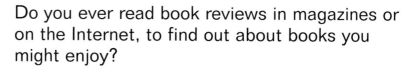

Do you ever read book reviews in magazines or on the Internet, to find out about books you might enjoy?

Here's a review of a children's book that was shortlisted for the *Guardian* Children's Book Award.

---

**The Fire-Eaters**
*by David Almond*
Hodder Children's Books

Set in 1950s Tyneside, in the build-up to the Cuban missile crisis, David Almond's novel shows what a subtle writer he is and how carefully and poetically he uses language.

As Bobby Burns turns 11, his life becomes more complicated. Not only does he have to face the new world of grammar school, with its arcane codes of behaviour and its bullying, but he is anxious about his sick father and has a growing awareness of social differences and the need to maintain friendships across them.

Almond makes familiar issues fresh; his characters are finely drawn and his depiction of place perfectly realised.

---

## Get ready

**1**  What does the beginning of the first paragraph tell the reader?

_____

**2**  What is the purpose of the second paragraph?

_____

**3**  What comments are made about the author's style?

_____

_____

**4**  Did the reviewer like the book?

_____

## Let's practise

Now write your own review.  Use this plan to organise your paragraphs, if it helps:

The setting of this book is _____

_____

_____

The plot is about _____

_____

_____

The author's style is _____

_____

My conclusion is _____

_____

_____

## Have a go

Read reviews of children's books in magazines and in newspapers. Do they express views both for and against? Do they make you want to read the book?

# 11: Write a cover blurb

A blurb on a book cover is different from a review, because it serves a different purpose. Its aim is to persuade you to buy and read the book.

Here's the blurb from the same book as in Unit 10, *The Fire-Eaters* by David Almond.

*There he was, below the bridge, half-naked, eyes blazing. He had a pair of burning torches. He ran them back and forth across his skin. He sipped from a bottle, breathed across a torch, and fire and fumes leapt from his lips. The air was filled with the scent of paraffin. He breathed again, a great high spreading flag of fire. He glared. He roared like an animal.*

That summer, life had seemed perfect for Bobby Burns. But now it's autumn and the winds of change are blowing hard. Bobby's dad is mysteriously ill. His new school is a cold and cruel place. And worse: nuclear war may be about to start. But Bobby has a wonder-working friend called Ailsa Spink. And he's found the fire-eater, a devil called McNulty. What can they do together on Bobby's beach? Is it possible to work miracles? Will they be able to transform the world?

**Get ready**

**1** Why is the first paragraph in italics?

_____

**2** What is the effect of the questions in the second paragraph?

_____

**3** Which did you find more persuasive: the book review or the cover blurb?

_____

## Let's practise

Write a new cover blurb for a book you've enjoyed. Remember the blurb has to sell the book, so it should be really positive – and short enough to fit on the back of the book! You could add some illustrations round the edge, to give an idea of the plot and the characters.

## Have a go

Look at the cover blurbs of books you've enjoyed. Could you improve on any of them? If so, you could send your blurb to the publisher of the book!

# 12: Write an advert

Have you ever listened to an advert on the radio? It's different from an advert on TV or in a magazine as there aren't any pictures. All the **persuasion** has to be in the words.

Read the example below: it's a radio advert for a new kind of umbrella. Can you see how each paragraph adds to the persuasion?

Do you hate rainy days? Do you hate going out with your old umbrella in the cold and the wet?

Well, here's a way of cheering up those splishy-splashy cold wet days. It will put a smile on your face, and a glow in your heart.

Our umbrellas are completely different. They have a heating filament in them, to keep your hands warm and your face aglow. Imagine those patio heaters beaming warmth down on your head. Well, these are just the same, but you carry them with you!

Where can you get hold of one of these amazing inventions? Go to our website, www.hotumbrellas.co.uk, and find out how to cheer up your winter days. You'll never walk alone again!

## Get ready

**1** What is the purpose of the first paragraph?

_____

**2** What does the second paragraph do?

_____

**3** What does the third paragraph do?

_____

**4** What is the purpose of the fourth paragraph?

_____

## Let's practise

Now we want you to invent a new everyday object, and write a radio advert for it. Follow the plan of four paragraphs, each serving a similar purpose to the model opposite.

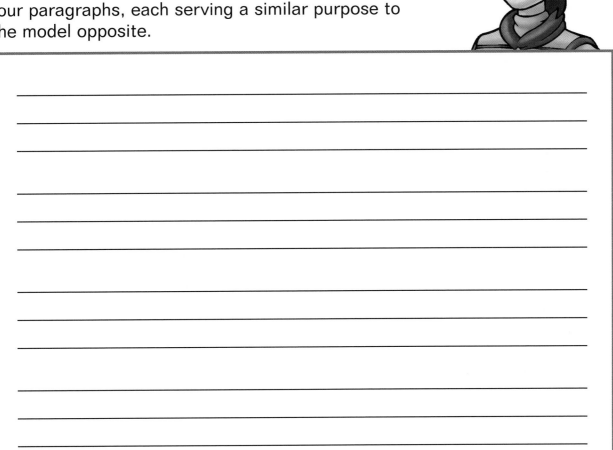

## Have a go

Did you enjoy the idea of inventing something new? The key thing is to identify a need, then try to answer the need. So think of a new service to offer on your mobile phone, and write an advert to persuade your friends of the benefits it could bring.

# 13: Write an explanation

Here's a real invention, which will save energy rather than wasting heat!

On the label there's an **explanation** of how the product works, written to help the people who've just bought it.

This explanation tells you how to use our special kettle, which is designed to be eco-friendly.

The special feature of this kettle is that it has two chambers, one to store water and one to heat water. You release water from one chamber into the other by pressing the special valve on the top of the kettle. Then you only heat the water you need!

So all you have to do to make this kettle work is fill the main chamber with enough water to see you through the morning. Then each time you want to heat water for a cup of coffee, press the valve to release enough water to heat that one cup.

The benefits are that it saves you water; it saves you time; it saves you energy.

## Get ready

**1** What tense is used for the verbs in the explanation?

_____

**2** What would have helped you to understand how it works?

_____

**3** Were you persuaded that it was a good idea? If so, what was it that persuaded you?

_____

## Let's practise

Now write your own explanation of how a particular gadget works in your home. Imagine your audience has never used this gadget before, but you have to use words not pictures to explain how it works.

This explanation tells you how _____

_____

The special feature _____

_____

_____

So all you have to do _____

_____

The benefits are _____

_____

## Have a go

Try inventing a new gadget for saving energy around the home. Write an explanation for the householder of how to use the gadget, and what the benefits are for the environment.

# 14: Write instructions

What's special about how instructions are written? Instructions **tell you what to do**, so rather than using the present tense as in an explanation, they use the command form of the verb: do this, check that, etc. We call this form of the verb the **imperative**.

**Instructions for flying**

**Wallace and Gromit's space capsule**

**What you need:**
Space suit
Ignition key
Map of outer space
Cheese supplies to last the journey

**What to do:**
1 Make sure your space suit has been thoroughly sterilised.
2 Store your cheese supplies in the fridge.
3 Check that you put the cat out before you lock the door.
4 Put the map on the ledge in front of you.
5 Fasten your seat belt.
6 Put the engine into gear.
7 Press the accelerator.
8 Count down and lift off!

## Get ready

**1** What are the two parts of the instructions?

_____

**2** What parts of speech are used for the two sections?

_____

**3** What punctuation is used for the two sections?

_____

## Let's practise

Your job is to write instructions for a team walking to the South Pole.

What will they need? What will they need to do to prepare for the journey?

What you need: _____

_____

_____

_____

What to do: _____

_____

_____

_____

_____

_____

## Have a go

Write instructions for your next family holiday. What does everyone need to take? What do they need to do to prepare for the journey?

# 15: Write a thesaurus entry

Do you know what a **thesaurus** is? It's like a dictionary, but rather than giving the meaning for each word, it gives you lots of other words that mean the same thing. This can really help with your writing.

Look at the entries below for three words beginning with **sh**:

---

**shiny** *adjective*
bright, gleaming, glossy, polished
*opposite* dull

**shiver** *verb*
to quiver, to shake, to shudder, to tremble

**shock** *verb*
1 to alarm, to frighten, to startle, to stun, to surprise
2 to disgust, to offend, to upset

---

## Get ready

**1** What comes after each word, in italics? _____

**2** Which kind of word is given an opposite meaning? _____

**3** Which word has two slightly different meanings? _____

**4** Choose one of the verbs, and use it in a sentence to show its meaning. _____

## Let's practise

Now we want you to fill in lists of words that mean the same as these key words.

**small** *adjective*

_____

*opposite* _____

**walk** *verb*

_____

**shout** *verb*

_____

## Have a go

Have you got a thesaurus at home? If not, see if you can take one home from school.

Then play a game with your family or friends, reading out words from the thesaurus, and seeing how many words everyone can list that mean the same.

We all know about using commas in lists. But it's also very common to use commas to separate off an 'aside', instead of using brackets.

Look at these examples. See how they must have punctuation at both the beginning and the end of the 'aside'.

```
Queen Elizabeth I, who came to the throne in
1558, reigned for 45 years.

My father, who had a terrible cold, sneezed
all day long.

The bird, sitting on the wire above our house,
had a beautiful song.

These two colours, red and blue, are always
the most popular.

The biggest actor (the one with the beard) had
the loudest voice.

The fat old cook — you should have seen him! —
could hardly fit into the kitchen.
```

## Get ready

Can you see that there's a slight difference between the examples?

- The ones with **commas** add extra information or an explanation, which is fairly essential to the sentence.

- Where you use **brackets**, the aside is less important, and could be missed out altogether.

- With **dashes**, the sense is quite informal, so you should avoid dashes in more formal writing.

Write some examples of these three kinds of punctuation. Make sure you include the closing punctuation mark as well as the opening one.

Commas _____

_____

_____

Brackets _____

_____

_____

Dashes _____

_____

_____

 **Have a go**

Look in your reading for examples of commas, brackets and dashes used for 'asides'.

# 17: Biography

Do you know the difference between autobiography and biography? **Autobiography** is when someone writes their own life story. **Biography** is when someone writes the story of someone else's life.

Here is an example of a short autobiography by a famous singer.

I was born in a small terraced house in the backstreets of Salford, near Manchester. My father was away travelling all the time, and my mother had to go out to work. So I was mainly brought up by my grandmother, who lived with us.

When I was at school, I was always mis-behaving. I wasn't good at lessons, and all I wanted to do was play music. I used to go off with my mates, and we'd practise in the basement of my friend Rod, who had a much bigger house than the rest of us.

What changed it all was when we left school. We sent a tape of one of our recordings to this record company. At first we heard nothing, so we started to give up on our chances. But then we were playing at a gig in Deansgate, and a guy came up to us after, saying he'd heard our tape and had come to hear what we were really like.

And I've never looked back since. We got a recording contract, and started travelling to all the big clubs round the country. Then I went solo, and you see my name around everywhere.

## Get ready

**1** How can you tell the singer is writing about his or her own life?

_____

**2** What tense are the verbs: past, present or future?

_____

**3** What period is the first paragraph about?

_____

**4** When was the turning point for this singer?

_____

## Let's practise

Try to turn this autobiography into a biography.

This means turning all the 'first person' writing into 'third person'. You'll also have to decide if the singer is male or female, and choose a name. You may need to continue on a separate piece of paper.

_____ was born in a small terraced house in the

backstreets of Salford, near Manchester. _____

_____

_____

_____

_____

_____

_____

_____

## Have a go

Write a brief version of your own autobiography. Plan out which event you'll cover in each photograph. Who will be your audience? How can you make them interested in your life?

What's special about newspaper writing?

It usually has to grab people's attention, and make them think about issues, because it's there to sell newspapers.

# Polar bears melt in the heat!

Should polar bears be kept in zoos in this scorching climate? How can we justify keeping them here?

Our reporter went down to the local zoo to see how the polar bears are coping in this heat. We have to admit that they are very well looked after. The keepers give them lots of care and attention, and give them their natural diet of fresh fish. And it does give us all the opportunity to see polar bears close up.

But the bears don't look happy in the heat. Their natural habitat is many degrees colder, and they are used to far more empty space. If we want children to see how these animals behave, there are plenty of nature films on television that we can all watch.

The zoo is organising an open day on 15 September, from 10a.m. to 3p.m., for schools to visit and ask the keepers about how they look after the animals. You are all welcome to come and give your views then!

## Get ready

Find these features in the newspaper article, and draw lines to link them to the text:

1    Headline to grab your attention

2    Leading questions to draw you in

3    Positive points of view in the first main paragraph

4    Opposing points of view in the next paragraph

5    Concluding paragraph of information

## Let's practise

Think of another controversial issue and write an article about it for your local newspaper.

Make sure you include a headline, leading questions, and separate paragraphs for the different points of view.

_____

_____     _____

_____     _____

_____     _____

_____     _____

_____     _____

_____     _____

_____     _____

_____     _____

_____     _____

_____     _____

_____     _____

## Have a go

Do you have a school newsletter or website that would welcome articles? Write a piece, with different points of view, to submit.

# 19: Argue a point of view

Have you ever written a letter about an issue you feel strongly about?

Here's what I wrote to the zoo after I read the newspaper article in Unit 18.

1 The Square,
Dunbarton DB1 3QX

21 August 2007

Dear Sir/Madam,

I want to write to you about the polar bears you keep in your zoo.

It has been so hot this summer that they must have been really suffering. I think that polar bears should live in their natural habitat, because they are suited to living on the ice and catching their fish from the sea.

I suppose there's an argument for letting the local children see what polar bears are really like. But if we want to see polar bears these days, we can see them on nature films.

Please tell me why you don't send your bears back to the habitat where they belong.

Yours truly,
Megan Griffiths

Fill in this grid with the reasons Megan gives for and against keeping polar bears in the zoo. Which list of reasons is longer?

| Against zoos | For zoos |
| --- | --- |
|  |  |
|  |  |
|  |  |
|  |  |

## Let's practise

Can you think of something in your neighbourhood that you feel strongly about?

Make a list of the points you want to make, as in the grid opposite.

Then write a letter, giving your reasoned point of view. And don't be too rude, or you won't get a reply!

## Have a go

Have you any strong views about wildlife? Try writing a letter to the World Wildlife Fund (WWF), clearly stating your points of view.

There are reasons why people use formal English for important texts. It's because the text has to look important, and the meaning has to be very clear.

Here is a set of rules that go out with the Key Stage 2 tests.

---

**Mark schemes for English tests**

1  The teacher's notes explain how pupils' answers will be marked.

2  The first guide is the 'assessment focus' sections, which describe what makes a good answer.

3  The notes then say how many marks can be awarded for different levels of answer.

4  They also give examples of pupils' handwritten answers, and explain how many marks should be given to each.

5  The marks are then converted to a scale of level 3 to level 5.

6  The tests are marked by external markers, following the mark schemes in these notes.

7  The results are sent to schools afterwards.

---

## Get ready

**1**  How are the rules laid out? _____

**2**  List any **passive** verb forms you can find. (For example, 'answers will be marked'.) _____

_____

_____

**3**  Who do you think is the audience for this text?

_____

## Let's practise

Now let's convert this into an informal explanation of how the tests are marked.

Imagine you're explaining to a friend how your tests will be marked. You'll want to change passive verbs into active verbs. We've given you a start . . .

I read in the teacher's notes how the markers are going to mark our tests.

They read the 'assessment focus' sections, to find out _____

_____

_____

_____

_____

_____

_____

_____

## Have a go

Write a list of notes to help the pupils in your school prepare for sitting the tests. What do they need to do before the tests, and what do they need to take with them?

Make the list quite formal, so that it can be put on the school noticeboard.

# How have I done?

**Quiz on writing**

Fill in one key feature for each of these kinds of writing:

1.  Limerick _____
2.  Playscript _____
3.  Direct speech _____
4.  Reported speech _____
5.  Story plan _____
6.  Fable _____
7.  Legend _____
8.  Shakespeare _____
9.  Book review _____
10. Cover blurb _____
11. Advert _____
12. Thesaurus _____
13. Autobiography _____
14. Explanation _____
15. Instructions _____
16. Newspaper article _____
17. Point of view _____
18. Formal English _____

**Quiz on punctuation**

Punctuate these sentences:

1. The king who was very old could not kneel down in his tight breeches

_____

2. He asked the queen could you help me please

_____

3. Not on your life she said

_____

4. I have it in mind to steal the throne if youre not up to it

_____

5. So without a pause she vaulted over the poor man and plonked herself on the throne

_____

6. The courtiers cried out whats all this

_____

7. They held a quick referendum or quiz would people prefer a king or a queen

_____

8. The result of the vote was six for the king and four for the queen

_____

9. So in the end the king got himself back on the throne in the nick of time

_____

10. Never mind he said to the queen. Better luck next time

_____

# Answers

**Unit 1** (pages 6 and 7)
1 Five lines
2 8, 8, 5 or 6, 5 or 6, 8
3 1, 2, 5; 3, 4
4 Lines 1 and 5

**Unit 2** (pages 8 and 9)
1 In italic in square brackets
2 Present tense
3 In capital letters
4 No
5 Usually the speech

**Unit 3** (pages 10 and 11)
1 Speech marks
2 Inside the speech marks
3 To introduce each new speech
4 Asked, replied

**Unit 6** (pages 16 and 17)
1 There was once . . .
2 So that each cub can behave in a different way
3 The lioness
4 'rather boring', 'fell into the river', 'hid behind a large cactus'
5 *Carefully does it. Fools rush in . . .*, etc.

**Unit 7** (pages 18 and 19)
1 They probably existed, because of all the legends about them.
2 Probably not, as his behaviour was so magical.
3 Bravery and honour
4 Gawain was spared three times, for the three times he'd resisted the green knight's wife.

**Unit 8** (pages 20 and 21)
Let's practise
Briefly, the Nurse is saying, "Don't mess her about!"

**Unit 10** (pages 24 and 25)
1 First paragraph starts by describing the setting.
2 Second paragraph describes the plot.
3 'what a subtle writer he is and how carefully and poetically he uses language'; 'Almond makes familiar issues fresh; his characters are finely drawn and his depiction of place perfectly realised.'
4 Yes, the reviewer liked the book.

**Unit 11** (pages 26 and 27)
1 Because it's a quote from the book
2 To involve you in how the plot might develop

**Unit 12** (pages 28 and 29)
1 First paragraph involves the reader
2 Second paragraph promises a solution to the problem of rainy days
3 Third paragraph provides technical explanation
4 Fourth paragraph tells you where to get hold of the product

**Unit 13** (pages 30 and 31)
1 Present tense
2 Probably a diagram would help

**Unit 14** (pages 32 and 33)
1 What you need; What to do
2 Nouns; imperative verbs
3 List, capital letters, no full stops; sentences with capital letters and full stops

**Unit 15** (pages 34 and 35)
1 The part of speech
2 The adjective
3 The verb 'shock'

**Unit 17** (pages 38 and 39)
1 The extract is written in the first person.
2 Past tense
3 Early family life
4 When they sent a tape to the record company and someone came to hear them play.

**Unit 19** (pages 42 and 43)
*Against*
Our climate is too hot for polar bears.
Animals should live in their natural habitat.
We can see animals on nature films.
*For*
Letting children see what polar bears look like

**Unit 20** (pages 44 and 45)
1 A numbered list
2 'marks can be awarded', 'marks should be given', 'marks are then converted', 'tests are marked', 'results are sent'
3 Teachers, and possibly parents

**How have I done?** (pages 46 and 47)
Quiz on writing
Any correct answer

Quiz on punctuation
1 The king, who was very old, could not kneel down in his tight breeches.
2 He asked the queen, "Could you help me, please?"
3 "Not on your life," she said.
4 "I have it in mind to steal the throne, if you're not up to it."
5 So, without a pause, she vaulted over the poor man and plonked herself on the throne.
6 The courtiers cried out, "What's all this?"
7 They held a quick referendum (or quiz). Would people prefer a king or a queen?
8 The result of the vote was six for the king and four for the queen.
9 So in the end the king got himself back on the throne, in the nick of time *or* So, in the end, the king got himself back on the throne, in the nick of time.
10 "Never mind," he said to the queen. "Better luck next time!"